The Key Facts™ on

Kazakhstan

Essential Information on Kazakhstan

By Patrick W. Nee

The Internationalist®

www.internationalist.com

The Internationalist®

International Business, Investment, and Travel

Published by:

The Internationalist Publishing Company

96 Walter Street/ Suite 200

Boston, MA 02131, USA

Tel: 617-354-7722

www.internationalist.com

PN@internationalist.com

Table Of Contents

Chapter 1: Background

Ethnic Kazakhs, a mix of Turkic and Mongol nomadic tribes who migrated to the region by the 13th century, were rarely united as a single nation. The area was conquered by Russia in the 18th century, and Kazakhstan became a Soviet Republic in 1936. During the 1950s and 1960s agricultural "Virgin Lands" program, Soviet citizens were encouraged to help cultivate Kazakhstan's northern pastures. This influx of immigrants (mostly Russians, but also some other deported nationalities) skewed the ethnic mixture and enabled non-ethnic Kazakhs to outnumber natives. Non-Muslim ethnic minorities departed Kazakhstan in large numbers from the mid-1990s through the mid-2000s and a national program has repatriated about a million ethnic Kazakhs back to Kazakhstan. These trends have allowed Kazakhs to become the titular majority again. This dramatic demographic shift has also undermined the previous religious diversity and made the country more than 70 percent Muslim. Kazakhstan's economy is larger than those of all the other Central Asian states largely due to the country's vast natural resources. Current issues include: developing a cohesive national identity; managing Islamic revivalism; expanding the development of the country's vast energy resources and exporting them to world markets; diversifying the economy outside the oil, gas, and mining sectors; enhancing Kazakhstan's economic competitiveness; developing a multiparty parliament and advancing political and social reform; and strengthening relations with neighboring states and other foreign powers.

Chapter 2: Geography

Location:

Central Asia, northwest of China; a small portion west of the Ural (Zhayyq) River in eastern-most Europe

Geographic coordinates:

48 00 N, 68 00 E

Map references:

Asia

Area:

total: 2,724,900 sq km

country comparison to the world: 9

land: 2,699,700 sq km

water: 25,200 sq km

Area - comparative:

slightly less than four times the size of Texas

Land boundaries:

total: 12,185 km

border countries: China 1,533 km, Kyrgyzstan 1,224 km, Russia 6,846 km, Turkmenistan 379 km, Uzbekistan 2,203 km

Coastline:

0 km (landlocked); note - Kazakhstan borders the Aral Sea, now split into two bodies of water (1,070 km), and the Caspian Sea (1,894 km)

Maritime claims:

none (landlocked)

Climate:

continental, cold winters and hot summers, arid and semiarid

Terrain:

vast flat steppe extending from the Volga in the west to the Altai Mountains in the east and from the plains of western Siberia in the north to oases and deserts of Central Asia in the south

Elevation extremes:

lowest point: Vpadina Kaundy -132 m

highest point: Khan Tangiri Shyngy (Pik Khan-Tengri) 6,995 m

Natural resources:

major deposits of petroleum, natural gas, coal, iron ore, manganese, chrome ore, nickel, cobalt, copper, molybdenum, lead, zinc, bauxite, gold, uranium

Land use:

arable land: 8.82%

permanent crops: 0.03%

other: 91.15% (2011)

Irrigated land:

20,660 sq km (2010)

Total renewable water resources:

107.5 cu km (2011)

Freshwater withdrawal (domestic/industrial/agricultural):

total: 21.14 cu km/yr (4%/30%/66%)

per capita: 1,304 cu m/yr (2010)

Natural hazards:

earthquakes in the south; mudslides around Almaty

Environment - current issues:

radioactive or toxic chemical sites associated with former defense industries and test ranges scattered throughout the country pose health risks for humans and animals; industrial pollution is severe in some cities; because the two main rivers that flowed into the Aral Sea have been diverted for irrigation, it is drying up and leaving behind a harmful layer of chemical pesticides and natural salts; these substances are then picked up by the wind and blown into noxious dust storms; pollution in the Caspian Sea; soil pollution from overuse of agricultural chemicals and salination from poor infrastructure and wasteful irrigation practices

Environment - international agreements:

party to: Air Pollution, Biodiversity, Climate Change, Desertification, Endangered Species, Environmental Modification, Hazardous Wastes, Ozone Layer Protection, Ship Pollution, Wetlands

signed, but not ratified: Climate Change-Kyoto Protocol

Geography - note:

landlocked; Russia leases approximately 6,000 sq km of territory enclosing the Baykonur Cosmodrome; in January 2004, Kazakhstan and Russia extended the lease to 2050

Chapter 3: People and Society

Nationality:

noun: Kazakhstani(s)

adjective: Kazakhstani

Ethnic groups:

Kazakh (Qazaq) 63.1%, Russian 23.7%, Uzbek 2.8%, Ukrainian 2.1%, Uighur 1.4%, Tatar 1.3%, German 1.1%, other 4.5% (2009 census)

Languages:

Kazakh (Qazaq, state language) 64.4%, Russian (official, used in everyday business, designated the "language of interethnic communication") 95% (2001 est.)

Religions:

Muslim 70.2%, Christian 26.2% (Russian Orthodox 23.9%, other Christian 2.3%), Buddhist 0.1%, other 0.2%, atheist 2.8%, unspecified 0.5% (2009 Census)

Population:

17,948,816 (July 2014 est.)

country comparison to the world: 62

Age structure:

0-14 years: 25.1% (male 2,247,628/female 2,254,744)

15-24 years: 16.1% (male 1,469,275/female 1,418,175)

25-54 years: 42.6% (male 3,720,498/female 3,927,626)

55-64 years: 7% (male 724,683/female 935,416)

65 years and over: 6.8% (male 429,565/female 821,206)

(2014 est.)

Dependency ratios:

total dependency ratio: 48 %

youth dependency ratio: 38.1 %

elderly dependency ratio: 9.9 %

potential support ratio: 10.1 (2013)

Median age:

total: 29.7 years

male: 28.4 years

female: 31.1 years (2014 est.)

Population growth rate:

1.17% (2014 est.)

country comparison to the world: 103

Birth rate:

19.61 births/1,000 population (2014 est.)

country comparison to the world: 88

Death rate:

8.31 deaths/1,000 population (2014 est.)

country comparison to the world: 89

Net migration rate:

0.42 migrant(s)/1,000 population (2014 est.)

country comparison to the world: 72

Urbanization:

urban population: 53.6% of total population (2011)

rate of urbanization: 0.87% annual rate of change (2010-15 est.)

Major urban areas - population:

Almaty 1.383 million; ASTANA (capital) 650,000 (2009)

Sex ratio:

at birth: 0.94 male(s)/female

0-14 years: 1 male(s)/female

15-24 years: 1.04 male(s)/female

25-54 years: 0.95 male(s)/female

55-64 years: 0.92 male(s)/female

65 years and over: 0.52 male(s)/female

total population: 0.92 male(s)/female (2014 est.)

Mother's mean age at first birth:

27.6 (2010 est.)

Maternal mortality rate:

51 deaths/100,000 live births (2010)

country comparison to the world: 107

Infant mortality rate:

    total: 21.61 deaths/1,000 live births

    country comparison to the world: 83

    male: 24.34 deaths/1,000 live births

    female: 19.06 deaths/1,000 live births (2014 est.)

Life expectancy at birth:

    total population: 70.24 years

    country comparison to the world: 150

    male: 64.98 years

    female: 75.17 years (2014 est.)

Total fertility rate:

    2.34 children born/woman (2014 est.)

    country comparison to the world: 92

Contraceptive prevalence rate:

    51% (2011)

Health expenditures:

    3.9% of GDP (2011)

    country comparison to the world: 165

Physicians density:

    3.84 physicians/1,000 population (2011)

Hospital bed density:

    7.6 beds/1,000 population (2009)

Drinking water source:

improved:

urban: 98.7% of population

rural: 90.4% of population

total: 94.8% of population

unimproved:

urban: 1.3% of population

rural: 9.6% of population

total: 5.2% of population (2011 est.)

Sanitation facility access:

improved:

urban: 96.8% of population

rural: 97.9% of population

total: 97.3% of population

unimproved:

urban: 3.2% of population

rural: 2.1% of population

total: 2.7% of population (2011 est.)

HIV/AIDS - adult prevalence rate:

0.1% (2012)

country comparison to the world: 153

HIV/AIDS - people living with HIV/AIDS:

13,000 (2012)

country comparison to the world: 96

HIV/AIDS - deaths:

fewer than 500 (2012)

country comparison to the world: 92

Obesity - adult prevalence rate:

23.7% (2008)

country comparison to the world: 74

Children under the age of 5 underweight:

3.7% (2011)

country comparison to the world: 100

Education expenditures:

3.1% of GDP (2009)

country comparison to the world: 138

Literacy:

definition: age 15 and over can read and write

total population: 99.7%

male: 99.8%

female: 99.7% (2009 est.)

School life expectancy (primary to tertiary education):

total: 15 years

male: 15 years

female: 15 years (2012)

Child labor – children ages 5-14:

total number: 59,254

percentage: 2% (2006 est.)

Unemployment, youth ages 15-24:

<u>total</u>: 3.9%

<u>country comparison to the world</u>: 139

<u>male</u>: 2.9%

<u>female</u>: 5.1% (2012)

Chapter 4: Government and Key Leaders

Country name:

conventional long form: Republic of Kazakhstan

conventional short form: Kazakhstan

local long form: Qazaqstan Respublikasy

local short form: Qazaqstan

former: Kazakh Soviet Socialist Republic

Government type:

republic; authoritarian presidential rule, with little power outside the executive branch

Capital:

name: Astana

geographic coordinates: 51 10 N, 71 25 E

time difference: UTC+6 (11 hours ahead of Washington, DC during Standard Time)

note: Kazakhstan is divided into two time zones

Administrative divisions:

14 provinces (oblystar, singular - oblys) and 3 cities* (qalalar, singular - qala); Almaty Oblysy, Almaty Qalasy*, Aqmola Oblysy (Astana), Aqtobe Oblysy, Astana Qalasy*, Atyrau Oblysy, Batys Qazaqstan Oblysy [West Kazakhstan] (Oral), Bayqongyr Qalasy [Baykonur]*, Mangghystau Oblysy (Aqtau), Ongtustik Qazaqstan Oblysy [South Kazakhstan] (Shymkent), Pavlodar Oblysy, Qaraghandy Oblysy, Qostanay Oblysy, Qyzylorda Oblysy,

Shyghys Qazaqstan Oblysy [East Kazakhstan] (Oskemen),
Soltustik Qazaqstan Oblysy [North Kazakhstan]
(Petropavlovsk), Zhambyl Oblysy (Taraz)
note: administrative divisions have the same names as
their administrative centers (exceptions have the
administrative center name following in parentheses); in
1995, the Governments of Kazakhstan and Russia entered
into an agreement whereby Russia would lease for a period
of 20 years an area of 6,000 sq km enclosing the Baykonur
space launch facilities and the city of Bayqongyr
(Baykonur, formerly Leninsk); in 2004, a new agreement
extended the lease to 2050

Independence:

16 December 1991 (from the Soviet Union)

National holiday:

Independence Day, 16 December (1991)

Constitution:

previous 1937, 1978 (preindependence); latest adopted 28
January 1993, approved by referendum 30 August 1995,
effective 5 September 1995; amended 1998, 2007, 2011
(2012)

Legal system:

civil law system influenced by Roman-Germanic law and
by the theory and practice of the Russian Federation

International law organization participation:

has not submitted an ICJ jurisdiction declaration; non-party state to the ICCt

Suffrage:

18 years of age; universal

Executive branch:

chief of state: President Nursultan Abishuly NAZARBAYEV (chairman of the Supreme Soviet from 22 February 1990, elected president 1 December 1991)

head of government: Prime Minister Tigran SARGSIAN (since 9 April 2008)

cabinet: Prime Minister Karim MASSIMOV (since 2 April 2014); First Deputy Prime Minister Bakytzhan SAGINTAYEV (since 16 January 2013); Deputy Prime Ministers Gulshara ABDYKHALIKOVA (since 28 November 2013), Aset ISEKESHEV (since 25 September 2012); Bakyt SULTANOV (since 6 November 2013)

elections: president elected by popular vote for a five-year term; election last held on 3 April 2011 (next to be held in 2016); prime minister and deputy prime ministers appointed by the president, with Mazhilis approval; note - constitutional amendments of May 2007 shortened the presidential term from seven years to five years and established a two-consecutive-term limit; NAZARBAYEV has official status as the "First President of Kazakhstan" and is allowed an unlimited amount of terms

note: constitutional amendments of February 2011 moved election date from 2012 to April 2011 but kept five-year term; subsequent election to take place in 2016

election results: Nursultan Abishuly NAZARBAYEV reelected president; percent of vote - Nursultan Abishuly NAZARBAYEV 95.5%, other 4.5%

Legislative branch:

bicameral Parliament consists of the Senate (47 seats; 15 members are appointed by the president; 32 members elected by local assemblies; members serve six-year terms, but elections are staggered with half of the members up for re-election every three years) and the Mazhilis (107 seats; 9 out of the 107 Mazhilis members elected by the Assembly of the People of Kazakhstan, a presidentially appointed advisory body designed to represent the country's ethnic minorities; non-appointed members are popularly elected to serve five-year terms)

elections: Senate - (indirect) last held in August 2011 (next to be held in 2014); Mazhilis - last held on 15 January 2012 (next to be held in 2017)

election results: Senate - percent of vote by party - NA; seats by party - Nur Otan 16; Mazhilis - percent of vote by party - Nur-Otan 81%, Ak Zhol 7.5%, Communist People's Party 7.2%, other 4.3%; seats by party - Nur-Otan 83, Ak Zhol 8, Communist People's Party 7

Judicial branch:

Highest court(s): Supreme Court of the Republic (consists of 44 members); Constitutional Council (consists of 7 members)

Judge selection and term of offfice: Supreme Court judges proposed by the president of ther epublic on recommendation of the Supreme Judicial Council, and confirmed by the Senate; judge tenure NA; Constitutional Council - the president of the republic, the Senate chairperson, the Majilis chairperson each appoints one member for a 3-year term and each appoints one member for a 6-year term; chairperson of the Constitutional Council appointed by the president of the republic for a 6-year term

subordinate courts: regional and local courts

Political parties and leaders:

Ak Zhol Party (Bright Path) [Azat PERUASHEV]

Alga [Vladimir KOZLOV] (unregistered and banned as extremist in November 2012)

Auyl (Village) [Gani KALIYEV]

Azat (Freedom) Party [Bolat ABILOV] (formerly True Ak Zhol Party)

Birlik (Unity) [Seril SULTANGALI] (Birlik is an April 2013 merger of Adilet (Justice; formerly Democratic Party of Kazakhstan) and Rukhaniyat (Spirituality))

NSDP [Zharmakhan TUYAKBAY]

Communist Party of Kazakhstan or KPK [Serikbolsyn ABDILDIN] (suspended by court decision)

Communist People's Party of Kazakhstan [Vladislav KOSAREV]

National Social Democratic Party or NSDP [Zharmakhan TUYAKBAY]

Nur Otan (Fatherland's Ray of Light) [Nursultan NAZARBAYEV, Nurlan NIGMATULIN] (the Agrarian, Asar, and Civic parties merged with Otan)

Patriots' Party [Gani KASYMOV]

Political pressure groups and leaders:

Adil-Soz [Tamara KALEYEVA]

Almaty Helsinki Committee [Ninel FOKINA]

Confederation of Free Trade Unions [Sergei BELKIN]

For Fair Elections [Yevgeniy ZHOVTIS, Sabit ZHUSUPOV, Sergey DUVANOV, Ibrash NUSUPBAYEV]

Kazakhstan International Bureau on Human Rights [Yevgeniy ZHOVTIS, Chairman of Bureau's Council, Roza AKYLBEKOVA, director]

Khalyk Maidany (Peoples' Front) - an informal union between the unregistered Alga Party, the unregistered

Communist Party of Kazakhstan, and several
opposition-oriented civil society groups, banned in
November 2012 [no formal leader]

Pan-National Social Democratic Party of Kazakhstan
[Zharmakhan TUYAKBAY]

Pensioners Movement or Pokoleniye [Irina
SAVOSTINA, chairwoman]

Republican Network of International Monitors
[Daniyar LIVAZOV]

Transparency International [Sergey ZLOTNIKOV]

International organization participation:

ADB, CICA, CIS, CSTO, EAEC, EAPC, EBRD, ECO,
EITI (candidate country), FAO, GCTU, IAEA, IBRD,
ICAO, ICC (NGOs), ICRM, IDA, IDB, IFAD, IFC,
IFRCS, ILO, IMF, IMO, Interpol, IOC, IOM, IPU, ISO,
ITSO, ITU, MIGA, NAM (observer), NSG, OAS
(observer), OIC, OPCW, OSCE, PFP, SCO, UN,
UNCTAD, UNESCO, UNIDO, UNWTO, UPU, WCO,
WFTU (NGOs), WHO, WIPO, WMO, WTO (observer),
ZC

Diplomatic representation in the US:

chief of mission: Ambassador Kayrat UMAROV (since 14
January 2013)

chancery: 1401 16th Street NW, Washington, DC 20036

telephone: [1] (202) 232-5488

FAX: [1] (202) 232-5845

consulate(s) general: New York

Diplomatic representation from the US:

chief of mission: Ambassador (vacant); Charge d'Affaires John ORDWAY

embassy: Rakhymzhan Koshkarbayev Ave. No 3, Astana 010010

mailing address: use embassy street address

telephone: [7] (7172) 70-21-00

FAX: [7] (7172) 54-09-14

Key Leaders:

Pres.	Nursultan NAZARBAYEV
Prime Min.	Serik AKHMETOV
First Dep. Prime Min.	Bakytzhan SAGINTAYEV
Dep. Prime Min.	Aset ISEKESHEV
Dep. Prime Min.	Yerbol ORYNBAYEV
Dep. Prime Min.	Bakyt SULTANOV
Min. of Agriculture	Asylzhan MAMYTBEKOV
Min. of Culture & Information	Mukhtar KUL-MUKHAMMED
Min. of Defense	Adilbek DZHAKSYBEKOV
Min. of Economic Integration	Zhanar AYTZHANOVA
Min. of Economy & Budget Planning	Yerbolat DOSAYEV
Min. of Education & Science	Aslan SARINZHIPOV
Min. of Emergency Situations	Vladimir BOZHKO
Min. of Environmental Protection	Nurlan KAPPAROV
Min. of Finance	Bakyt SULTANOV
Min. of Foreign Affairs	Yerlan IDRISOV
Min. of Health	Salidat KAIRBEKOVA

Min. of Industry & New Technologies	Aset ISEKESHEV
Min. of Internal Affairs	Kalmukhanbet KASYMOV
Min. of Justice	Berik IMASHEV
Min. of Labor & Social Protection	Tamara DUYSENOVA
Min. of Oil & Gas	Uzakbay KARABALIN
Min. of Regional Development	Bolat ZHAMISHEV
Min. of Transport & Communications	Askar ZHUMAGALIYEV
Sec. of the Security Council	Kayrat KOZHAMZHAROV
Chmn., Ctte. for National Security (KNB)	Nurtay ABYKAYEV
Chmn., National Bank	Kayrat KELIMBETOV
Ambassador to the US	Kayrat UMAROV
Permanent Representative to the UN, New York (Acting)	Akan RAKHMETULIN

Flag description:

a gold sun with 32 rays above a soaring golden steppe eagle, both centered on a sky blue background; the hoist side displays a national ornamental pattern "koshkar-muiz" (the horns of the ram) in gold; the blue color is of religious significance to the Turkic peoples of the country, and so symbolizes cultural and ethnic unity; it also represents the endless sky as well as water; the sun, a source of life and energy, exemplifies wealth and plenitude; the sun's rays are shaped like grain, which is the basis of abundance and prosperity; the eagle has appeared on the flags of Kazakh tribes for centuries and represents freedom, power, and the flight to the future

National symbol(s):

golden eagle

National anthem:

name: "Menin Qazaqstanim" (My Kazakhstan)

lyrics/music: Zhumeken NAZHIMEDENOV and Nursultan NAZARBAYEV/Shamshi KALDAYAKOV

note: adopted 2006; President Nursultan NAZARBAYEV played a role in revising the lyrics

Chapter 5: Economy

Economy - overview:

Kazakhstan, geographically the largest of the former Soviet republics, excluding Russia, possesses enormous fossil fuel reserves and plentiful supplies of other minerals and metals, such as uranium, copper, and zinc. It also has a large agricultural sector featuring livestock and grain. In 2002 Kazakhstan became the first country in the former Soviet Union to receive an investment-grade credit rating. Extractive industries have been and will continue to be the engine of Kazakhstan's growth, although the country is aggressively pursuing diversification strategies. Landlocked, with restricted access to the high seas, Kazakhstan relies on its neighbors to export its products, especially oil and grain. Although its Caspian Sea ports, pipelines, and rail lines carrying oil have been upgraded, civil aviation and roadways continue to need attention. Telecoms are improving, but require considerable investment, as does the information technology base. Supply and distribution of electricity can be erratic because of regional dependencies, but the country is moving forward with plans to improve reliability of electricity and gas supply to its population. At the end of 2007, global financial markets froze up and the loss of capital inflows to Kazakhstani banks caused a credit crunch. The subsequent and sharp fall of oil and commodity prices in 2008 aggravated the economic situation, and Kazakhstan plunged into recession. While the global financial crisis took a significant toll on Kazakhstan's economy, it has rebounded well, helped by prudent government measures. Rising commodity prices have helped the recovery. Despite solid macroeconomic indicators, the government realizes that its economy suffers from an overreliance on oil and extractive industries, the so-called "Dutch disease." In response, Kazakhstan has embarked on an ambitious diversification program, aimed at developing targeted sectors like transport, pharmaceuticals, telecommunications, petrochemicals and food processing. In 2010 Kazakhstan joined the Belarus-Kazakhstan-Russia Customs Union in an effort to boost foreign investment and improve trade relationships.

GDP (purchasing power parity):

$243.6 billion (2013 est.)

country comparison to the world: 53

$231.9 billion (2012 est.)

$220.6 billion (2011 est.)

note: data are in 2013 US dollars

GDP (official exchange rate):

$224.9 billion (2013 est.)

GDP - real growth rate:

5% (2013 est.)

country comparison to the world: 60

5.1% (2012 est.)

7.5% (2011 est.)

GDP - per capita (PPP):

$14,100 (2013 est.)

country comparison to the world: 95

$13,700 (2012 est.)

$13,200 (2011 est.)

note: data are in 2013 US dollars

Gross national saving:

28.8% of GDP (2013 est.)

country comparison to the world: 30

23.9% of GDP (2012 est.)

28.4% of GDP (2011 est.)

GDP – composition, by end use:

household consumption: 51%

government consumption: 12.4%

investment in fixed capital: 22.1%

investment in inventories: 2.5%

exports of goods and services: 44.6%

imports of goods and services: --32.6% (2013 est.)

GDP - composition by sector:

agriculture: 5.2%

industry: 37.9%

services: 56.9% (2011 est.)

Agriculture – products:

grain (mostly spring wheat and barley), potatoes, vegetables, melons; livestock

Industries:

oil, coal, iron ore, manganese, chromite, lead, zinc, copper, titanium, bauxite, gold, silver, phosphates, sulfur, uranium, iron and steel; tractors and other agricultural machinery, electric motors, construction materials

Industrial production growth rate:

2.1% (2013 est.)

country comparison to the world:123

Labor force:

9.022 million (2013 est.)

country comparison to the world: 52

Labor force - by occupation:

agriculture: 25.8%

industry: 11.9%

services: 62.3% (2012)

Unemployment rate:

5.3% (2013 est.)

country comparison to the world: 51

5.3% (2012 est.)

Population below poverty line:

5.3% (2011 est.)

Household income or consumption by percentage share:

lowest 10%: 3.9%

highest 10%: 23.7% (2011 est.)

Distribution of family income - Gini index:

28.9 (2011)

country comparison to the world: 122

31.5 (2003)

Budget:

revenues: $43.88 billion

expenditures: $49 billion (2013 est.)

Taxes and other revenues:

19.5% of GDP (2013 est.)

country comparison to the world: 170

Budget surplus (+) or deficit (-):

2.3% of GDP (2013 est.)

country comparison to the world: 94

Public debt:

15.6% of GDP (2013 est.)

country comparison to the world: 142

13.2% of GDP (2012 est.)

Inflation rate (consumer prices):

5.8% (2013 est.)

country comparison to the world: 165

5.1% (2012 est.)

Central bank discount rate:

5.5% (31 December 2012 est.)

country comparison to the world: 36

7.5% (31 December 2011 est.)

Commercial bank prime lending rate:

6.3% (31 December 2013 est.)

country comparison to the world: 132

6.6% (31 December 2012 est.)

Stock of narrow money:

$24.51 billion (31 December 2013 est.)

country comparison to the world: 63

$25.82 billion (31 December 2012 est.)

Stock of broad money:

$70.36 billion (31 December 2012 est.)

country comparison to the world: 62

$65.71 billion (31 December 2011 est.)

Stock of domestic credit:

$87.05 billion (31 December 2013 est.)

country comparison to the world: 56

$83.08 billion (31 December 2012 est.)

Market value of publicly traded shares:

$23.5 billion (31 December 2012 est.)

country comparison to the world: 53

$43.3 billion (31 December 2011)

$60.74 billion (31 December 2010 est.)

Current account balance:

$1.965 billion (2013 est.)

country comparison to the world: 42

$640.5 million (2012 est.)

Exports:

$87.23 billion (2013 est.)

country comparison to the world: 43

$86.93 billion (2012 est.)

Exports - commodities:

oil and oil products, natural gas, ferrous metals, chemicals, machinery, grain, wool, meat, coal

Exports - partners:

China 19.3%, Italy 18.1%, Netherlands 8.8%, France 6.6%, Switzerland 5.8%, Austria 5.8% (2012)

Imports:

$52.03 billion (2013 est.)

country comparison to the world: 55

$49.08 billion (2012 est.)

Imports - commodities:

machinery and equipment, metal products, foodstuffs

Imports - partners:

China 28%, Ukraine 10.9%, Germany 8.5%, US 7.9% (2012)

Reserves of foreign exchange and gold:

$29.34 billion (31 December 2013 est.)

country comparison to the world: 53

$28.28 billion (31 December 2012 est.)

Debt - external:

$131.3 billion (31 December 2013 est.)

country comparison to the world: 41

$133.5 billion (31 December 2012 est.)

Exchange rates:

tenge (KZT) per US dollar -

151.8 (2013 est.)

149.11 (2012 est.)

147.36 (2010 est.)

147.5 (2009)

120.25 (2008)

Chapter 6: Energy

Electricity - production:

> 90.53 billion kWh (2012 est.)

> country comparison to the world: 36

Electricity - consumption:

> 88.11 billion kWh (2011 est.)

> country comparison to the world: 33

Electricity - exports:

> 1.8 billion kWh (2011 est.)

> country comparison to the world: 43

Electricity - imports:

> 3.7 billion kWh (2011 est.)

> country comparison to the world: 43

Electricity - installed generating capacity:

> 18.73 million kW (2010 est.)

> country comparison to the world: 39

Electricity - from fossil fuels:

> 88.2% of total installed capacity (2010 est.)

> country comparison to the world: 81

Electricity - from nuclear fuels:

> 0% of total installed capacity (2010 est.)

> country comparison to the world: 121

Electricity - from hydroelectric plants:

> 11.8% of total installed capacity (2010 est.)

> country comparison to the world: 110

Electricity - from other renewable sources:

0% of total installed capacity (2010 est.)

country comparison to the world: 190

Crude oil - production:

1.606 million bbl/day (2012 est.)

country comparison to the world: 18

Crude oil - exports:

1.406 million bbl/day (2010 est.)

country comparison to the world: 12

Crude oil - imports:

119,600 bbl/day (2010 est.)

country comparison to the world: 47

Crude oil - proved reserves:

30 billion bbl (1 January 2013 es)

country comparison to the world: 11

Refined petroleum products - production:

288,600 bbl/day (2010 est.)

country comparison to the world: 43

Refined petroleum products - consumption:

244,200 bbl/day (2011 est.)

country comparison to the world: 52

Refined petroleum products - exports:

149,800 bbl/day (2011 est.)

country comparison to the world: 38

Refined petroleum products - imports:

94,430 bbl/day (2010 est.)

country comparison to the world:52

Natural gas - production:

20.2 billion cu m (2011 est.)

country comparison to the world: 31

Natural gas - consumption:

10.2 billion cu m (2011 est.)

country comparison to the world: 45

Natural gas - exports:

9.7 billion cu m (2011 est.)

country comparison to the world: 25

Natural gas - imports:

10.7 billion cu m (2011 est.)

country comparison to the world: 28

Natural gas - proved reserves:

2.407 trillion cu m (1 January 2013 es)

country comparison to the world: 14

Carbon dioxide emissions from consumption of energy:

195.4 million Mt (2011 est.)

country comparison to the world: 30

Chapter 7: Communications

Telephones - main lines in use:

4.34 million (2012)

country comparison to the world: 40

Telephones - mobile cellular:

28.731 million (2012)

country comparison to the world: 37

Telephone system:

general assessment: inherited an outdated

telecommunications network from the Soviet era requiring

modernization

domestic: intercity by landline and microwave radio relay;

number of fixed-line connections is gradually increasing

and fixed-line teledensity now roughly 25 per 100 persons;

mobile-cellular usage has increased rapidly and the

subscriber base now exceeds 140 per 100 persons

international: country code - 7; international traffic with

other former Soviet republics and China carried by

landline and microwave radio relay and with other

countries by satellite and by the Trans-Asia-Europe (TAE)

fiber-optic cable; satellite earth stations - 2 Intelsat (2008)

Broadcast media:

state owns nearly all radio and TV transmission facilities

and operates national TV and radio networks; nearly all

nationwide TV networks are wholly or partly owned by

the government; some former state-owned media outlets have been privatized; households with satellite dishes have access to foreign media; a small number of commercial radio stations operate along with state-run radio stations; recent legislation requires all media outlets to register with the government and all TV providers to broadcast in digital format by 2015 (2008)

Internet country code:

.kz

Internet hosts:

67,464 (2012)

country comparison to the world: 90

Internet users:

5.299 million (2009)

country comparison to the world: 44

Chapter 8: Transportation

Airports:

> 96 (2013)
>
> <u>country comparison to the world</u>: 60

Airports - with paved runways:

> <u>total</u>: 63
>
> <u>over 3,047 m</u>: 10
>
> <u>2,438 to 3,047 m</u>: 25
>
> <u>1,524 to 2,437 m</u>: 15
>
> <u>914 to 1,523 m</u>: 5
>
> <u>under 914 m</u>: 8 (2013)

Airports - with unpaved runways:

> <u>total</u>: 33
>
> <u>over 3,047 m</u>: 5
>
> <u>2,438 to 3,047 m</u>: 7
>
> <u>1,524 to 2,437 m</u>: 3
>
> <u>914 to 1,523 m</u>: 5
>
> <u>under 914 m</u>: 13 (2013)

Heliports:

> 3 (2013)

Pipelines:

> condensate 658 km; gas 12,432 km; oil 11,313 km; refined products 1,095 km; water 1,465 km (2013)

Railways:

> total: 15,333 km
>
> country comparison to the world: 18
>
> broad gauge: 15,333 km 1.520-m gauge (4,000 km electrified) (2012)

Roadways:

> total: 97,418 km
>
> country comparison to the world: 18
>
> paved: 87,140 km
>
> unpaved: 10,278 km (2012)

Waterways:

> 4,000 km (on the Ertis (Irtysh) River (80%) and Syr Darya (Syrdariya) River) (2010)
>
> country comparison to the world: 27

Merchant marine:

> total: 11
>
> country comparison to the world: 111
>
> by type: cargo 1, petroleum tanker 8, refrigerated cargo 1, specialized tanker 1
>
> foreign-owned: 3 (Austria 1, Ireland 1, Turkey 1) (2010)

Ports and terminals:

> major seaport(s): Aqtau (Shevchenko), Atyrau (Gur'yev)
>
> river port(s): Oskemen (Ust-Kamenogorsk), Pavlodar, Semey (Semipalatinsk) (Irtysh River)

Chapter 9: Military

Military branches:

Kazakhstan Armed Forces: Ground Forces, Navy, Air Mobile Forces, Air Defense Forces (2013)

Military service age and obligation:

18 is the legal minimum age for compulsory military service; conscript service obligation is 2 years, but Kazakhstan may be transitioning to a contract force; 19 is the legal minimum age for voluntary service; military cadets in intermediate (ages 15-17) and higher (ages 17-21) education institutes are classified as military service personnel (2012)

Manpower available for military service:

males age 16-49: 4,163,629

females age 16-49: 4,179,051 (2010 est.)

Manpower fit for military service:

males age 16-49: 2,909,999

females age 16-49: 3,528,169 (2010 est.)

Manpower reaching militarily significant age annually:

male: 125,322

female: 119,541 (2010 est.)

Military expenditures:

1.21% of GDP (2012)

country comparison to the world: 84

0.97% of GDP (2011)

1.21% of GDP (2010)

Chapter 10: Transnational Issues

Disputes - international:

Kyrgyzstan has yet to ratify the 2001 boundary delimitation with Kazakhstan; field demarcation of the boundaries commenced with Uzbekistan in 2004 and with Turkmenistan in 2005; ongoing demarcation with Russia began in 2007; demarcation with China was completed in 2002; creation of a seabed boundary with Turkmenistan in the Caspian Sea remains under discussion; Azerbaijan, Kazakhstan, and Russia ratified Caspian seabed delimitation treaties based on equidistance, while Iran continues to insist on a one-fifth slice of the sea

Refugees and internally displaced persons:

stateless persons: 6,935 (2012)

Illicit drugs:

significant illicit cultivation of cannabis for CIS markets, as well as limited cultivation of opium poppy and ephedra (for the drug ephedrine); limited government eradication of illicit crops; transit point for Southwest Asian narcotics bound for Russia and the rest of Europe; significant consumer of opiates

Map of Kazakhstan

Other Key Facts™ Titles

Key Facts on South Korea

Key Facts on France

Key Facts on the United Kingdom

Key Facts on Egypt

Key Facts on Israel

All Key Facts™ Titles are Available at

www.Amazon.com

THE INTERNATIONALIST®

2014

WWW.INTERNATIONALIST.COM

www.ingramcontent.com/pod-product-compliance
Lightning Source LLC
Chambersburg PA
CBHW071807200526
45167CB00017B/1447